Angel on My Shoulder

Volume II

by Val Conlon

The notebooks published by us are private revelation to John Morgan.

But as publisher, in printing these notebooks, we are in complete conformity with the Church in accordance with the decrees of Pope Urban VIII respecting private revelations.

Pope Urban VIII decreed that the reader should always exercise prudence where alleged supernatural phenomena not attested to by the Church, is concerned.

However his holiness, also gave leadership in the matter of private revelations, when he stated:

"In cases which concern private revelations, it is better to believe than not to believe, for if you believe, and it is proven false, you will still receive all the blessing as if it had been true, because you believed it to be true."

Startling

Sensational

Bestseller

Volume II

(*over 50,000 copies of Vol I sold*)

Written and Published by Val Conlon

Divine Mercy Publications
Maryville, Skerries, Co. Dublin, **Ireland**
Tel: 00 353 1 8491458 Fax: 00 353 1 8492466
Email: info@divinemercy.org

www.divinemercy.org
www.hudt.org

The Phenomenon described by John Morgan

A few years ago a man, who introduced himself to me as Paul Kelly, said someone he knew wanted to see me. I asked him who exactly wanted to see me and what it was about. He gave me the name of a man, told me where he lived, and said it was in connection with the work that I do. I asked him for more information, but he said he would not like to say any more just to say that he thought what this man had to say was worthwhile listening to. He was sure I would be very interested, and it would be better if I saw the man myself.

He told me the man was not prepared to discuss it over the phone and would only speak to me in person. I was reluctant to see someone in such circumstances, not knowing what it was all about, but a few weeks later, curiosity got the better of me and I found myself going on a journey to meet this man at his home just as he had requested.

One Saturday I arranged to meet with Paul Kelly, who lived a four hour journey from me, at his home, and then we would go together to the other man's house where he would introduce us to each other. I parked outside Paul's home, and we walked the short distance to his neighbour. It was a beautiful day and as we walked down this country lane, I was taken by the beauty of the countryside I saw all around me, it was like God's own country. I heard sounds that I hadn't heard since I was a boy, crows screeching high on the tree tops, a horse neighing in the distance. I could even hear cattle munching grass in the fields on one side of the lane. On the other side there was no sign of life, only flat grass land stretching into the distance with a scarlet red corrugated hay haggard just in view on the horizon.

The tree tops on each side of the lane touched and seemed to caress, where the foliage met, creating a leafy green roof where the sun seemed to shoot through now and again, as we walked.

Just as we reached the turn into the entrance gateway of the house, a be-capped man on a bicycle passed by with a greeting of "Gomorra men", this was not a greeting that you would hear on the streets of Dublin, which left me in no doubt that I was in the heart of the countryside, and a long way from the city I had left that morning.

As we passed through the gate I discovered it was a thatched cottage the man lived in, and when we met the man who was introduced as John, I could see he was as rustic looking as the landscape all around him. Paul introduced us then said, "sure I'll leave ye to it, I'll come back in about an hour or so", and off he went.

John Morgan said, "come in and take the weight off yer legs". As we went in and he motioned me to a fireside chair, very properly named in the circumstances, as it was beside a bright coal lit fire, which surprised me a little as it was such a pleasant day outside. He must have sensed my surprise as he proceeded to explain that he lived alone and always kept a small fire going for company.

As he lowered himself into the seat he picked up a poker from beside the hearth and leaning towards the fire, began to improve the flame.

He didn't exactly poke the fire, but just moved the coals about a bit and seemed maybe to be just engaging himself, as he gathered his thoughts together to begin to speak. As the flame began to rise a little, it lit up a rugged weather beaten face that had seen a lot of outdoor life. It was not a young face and I guessed he must have been nearing eighty. My guess was not far out as he began to talk by saying as by way of introduction:

"I am eighty four years of age, and I've worked the land all my life". He paused as he continued to push coals around the fire. I sensed there was a shyness, which was holding him back from what ever was on his mind. Then he looked up again and said, "I've had an experience which I want to tell someone about, in fact not just one experience, but many".

Another pause as if he was not sure or still slightly embarrassed by what he wanted to disclose whatever it was. So I thought I had better engage in the conversation to help him get over his initial embarrassment of what ever it was he wanted to disclose to me.

I said, "John I don't know yet what you want to talk to me about or what kind of experience you have had, but I'm curious to know where you got my name, and as we obviously have never met before, how and why did you choose me to speak to me". For the first time since we sat down he looked me straight in the face and said, "it was because of an article you wrote on angels, which seemed to me like you had a personal experience, did you"? he asked.

John" I said, "you tell me why I am here and what your experience is, and then we'll talk about me, if your story warrants it". "Well" he began, "I have

never spoken to a soul except my friend Paul about this, and even that was very little just to say I had a vision, but my continued sanity forces me to tell someone the whole story.

I have read a lot of your articles and when I read the one you wrote about angels, I decided you were the one I would tell, you wrote about an experience you had in "San Giovanni" it was about the Archangel St. Michael, and that decided me to tell you". I said, "yes, I remember, that was a number of years ago, John".

Yes but it has taken me a long time to get up the courage to tell anyone" "O.K. John" I said getting a little impatient, "what exactly do you want to tell me"

Well" he said, "you see I have had many visits from an angel and I have it all written down in old notebooks". A silence ensued, as I was slightly taken aback, and he noticed and awaited a reaction in words from me. Turning this extraordinary revelation over in my mind, I thought to myself, the man certainly did not impress me as one of the many people that I have come across, who after about five minutes in their presence, you know are suffering from either a bout of schizophrenia, or over-fertile imaginations, and should really be in a more secure place.

People who I have dismissed by saying (and I'm sure priests will not thank me for this) but to conclude such a meeting I would comment "that's very fascinating, but I really think you should be telling a priest about it".

This man was not one of those, but yet I was reserving judgment. "How do you know it was an angel John?" I said, "Because he told me so" said John, "and he was all in white" I was still very apprehensive and wanted to ask questions that might prove to me that he wasn't as sensible as he looked.

W here exactly did you see him for the first time? Did he come in the gate, knock at your door, how did you first see him?" I asked.

H e first appeared to me one evening in the garden. Come on I'll show you", he said as he rose and asked me to go with him into the garden. I followed him and went around to the side of the house; he stopped at an old garden seat beneath a tree. "This is my favourite spot in the garden, this is the place where I sit on a nice evening after I've had my evening meal, smoke my pipe, and ponder life".

A s I looked all around, you could not see a house or dwelling of any kind in any direction, only the red corrugated barn in the distance that I had seen as I came down the lane. Behind the tree there was a neat well groomed back garden, with flowers hugging a timber rail fence that continued around the garden marking the boundary to the house area, and finishing at the gate pillar that held the entrance gate I had come through about half an hour before.

D o you take a drink John", I asked feeling slightly embarrassed having asked in such a pointed way, without being more subtle or diplomatic. John smiled at the obvious insinuation in the question. He was now seated on the old garden seat, in his favourite spot in the garden. "I don't", he said,

I used to have a pint in the evenings when I was younger, but I gave it up more than ten years ago when I could no longer walk to the pub with comfort, or maybe it was coming back, to be more precise, the old legs you know, they say they are the first thing to go as you get older, and I can surely confirm that".

Sorry John", I said, "I just want to eliminate anything that might have clouded your judgment".

I was becoming more interested in John's story as we talked because he was very ordinary, very calm, and certainly not putting himself forward as someone special, which of course he was, if this really happened. So I asked him to tell me the whole story from the beginning.

Well" said John, "It was right here on a summers evening just like this, I was smoking my pipe just gazing out at the countryside, when I sensed someone or something just behind me, I turned around and there as large as life was a smiling angel". "How did you know immediately he was an angel?" I asked.

Well that's the strange thing about it, I was not a bit frightened and I just knew it was an angel. Normally if someone came quietly up behind me that I didn't see coming, and appeared out of nowhere, it would frighten the life out of me, but he didn't, and by some interior knowledge that I didn't know existed, I just knew it was an angel".

I began to talk to him (the angel) as casually as if it was an ordinary stranger, "who are you", I said to him?

I am your guardian angel, and the reason that I am here is in answer to your questions".

Surprised I said "what questions?" "The questions you have been asking in your innermost private thoughts for the last thirty-three years, about God, about eternity, and the whole meaning of life".

The first thought I should have had I suppose, was that this was ridiculous, I'm talking to an angel, but it wasn't, it all seemed so normal sitting here talking to my Guardian angel, as if I was talking to my best friend.

I said, to him (the angel) "You're talking about fleeting thoughts I've had over the past thirty years". "Thirty-three years to be precise" said the angel, "and they may have been fleeting or occasional rather than continuing, but lets say they were recurring thoughts over a long period of time".

But why" I asked "after all these years are you only coming to me now?" "Because exactly thirty-three years ago you asked an interior question, it was, I wonder is there really a God. It was not an idle rhetorical question; it was a sincere plea from the heart.

That was the beginning of your spiritual life". "What?" I said, "surely that was evidence of my unbelief, how could that be something spiritual?"

Because John that was the beginning of your search, and you have been searching ever since, by continually asking questions, sometimes finding answers within yourself, but most of the time not. And on the thirty third anniversary of your first real interest in God, I as your guardian angel am allowed to appear to you, and audibly help you".

But I do believe", John said, "I go to Mass every Sunday, and I go to confession two or three times a year, and to the best of my knowledge I have not committed a mortal sin in the past twenty years".

John, that is not belief, that is insurance, most of your life you attended the sacraments because this is what you were brought up to do. You attended, but it was more a tradition in your life rather than a conviction, and you know deep within your own mind you still ponder that same question, does God really exist.

But your continuous pondering of your faith is a continuous search for the truth, and those that are sincerely searching for the truth, can be saved in that search. I am your guardian angel and there is no one that knows you better than I, except God. I am at your shoulder every moment of your life, and I can go inside your mind when I want to.

I can never interfere with any of your intentions or decisions, unless you ask my help, but I can interfere when in many cases you are inadvertently going to do something that could be dangerous to your life, and to your eternal soul".

B ut" I intervened, "I can understand inadvertently endangering my life, but how can you inadvertently endanger your soul?".

W ell let me give you an example, suppose you were day dreaming and step off the footpath in front of a bus, and since your last confession you have offended God, but maybe have not had the time because of a busy life to think about confession or repentance, I can pull you up in the nick of time, because at that moment you are endangering your life, and your soul".

I thought of all the times in my life that I had come close to having a serious accident and just by the grace of God it seemed, somehow escaped in the nick of time, especially on the old tractor, now I knew how. When he revealed this, it all made sense to me.

I was still pondering this and finally when I turned to ask another question, he was gone, without any warning. I was surprised and disappointed, but as I got up from the seat a neighbour was coming in the gate and I thought, maybe that's why he left so suddenly.

T hat said John, was the first experience I had, and that night when the neighbour was gone, I went inside and for some reason decided to write it all down, and I have written everything down that

passed between us since then. I think it is easier to show you the notebooks and let you read all of the questions I asked the angel about present day life and his answers, it's all in these notebooks. He then went into the house and came back with a big box of old notebooks which he handed me.

The angel visited John many times thereafter, and after each visit had finished John wrote it all down in these notebooks.

What follows in this book is the story of these visits and the conversations that followed between John Morgan, an Irish farmer and Seraph, a friendly angel from another world.

To save continuous explanation of who is speaking we have put John's questions to the angel in bold text, and the angels words are written in plain text.

The notebooks do not always give a date or time of a specific visit or occasion, so the conversations may not be in chronological order.

The angel starts off on this occasion by asking John:

Why do you think you are a bad person, is it because you question belief in God?

I have always had doubts, but I suppose it was mixed with a fear that if I allowed myself to believe I couldn't live up to what God expected of me. I suppose also I questioned that if God made me, why did he make me so imperfect.

What made you think you were imperfect John? Unfortunately I think you fell into a familiar trap of Satan's. He instills that first thought of imperfection and inadequacy into your mind and develops this thought process to a stage where you feel you are too bad to measure up to what God expects of you, and so you just give up in believing in God. Then he leaves you alone.

You must first understand, John, that life on earth is not a long difficult journey in the service of God.

God knows because you're human, that everything you do will not be perfect, humans are imperfect beings, and this is what all humans battle against on earth.

But simple acts of good, and obedience to your conscience are taken by God as a obedience to Him and therefore atonement for your imperfections.

But what if you are continuously falling and making errors?

God knows about human weakness and that you will fall from perfect grace continually, but as long as it is not deliberate or malicious, then good actions that are not specifically carried out as atonement, are taken as acts of atonement by God for these imperfections.

So each time you do something good or caring you are redressing the balance.

God will always take into account the good things that you do from the heart and set them against the things that you do that are not correct. Acts of goodness that you do for others are always taken as atonement.

Even when you acknowledge after the event something that you recognise as being wrong and feel sorry that you did it, that can be taken as atonement by God.

Do you mean God understands our sinning?

Always remember God loves you, that's why you're alive. He knows your imperfect, He also knows you inherited these imperfections. You may not always overcome your human failings but your efforts to overcome them are what is important.

God understands and pardons human frailty. The cry of a human soul never goes unheard with God.

Do you mean we should ask God for forgiveness outside of going to confession?

If you acknowledge your failings and your shortcomings and offer your efforts to overcome them, to God, the results of those efforts can change your life. One genuine act of faithfulness to God can atone for many sins. Acts of perfection are always taken as acts of atonement for imperfections.

Another thing I always felt it hard to do was to give an account of my sins to another human being. I think it was my pride. Should I have sought help somewhere to change my attitude to pride? How could I have changed that?

You must learn to understand yourself first. To know yourself you don't need advice from anyone. The beginning of all change must come from within your self. Look to your inner self. The answers lie within. You must allow your "God-given" inner being, your spirit, to influence your life.

I have never had many friends that I could measure myself against or seek approval from.

Stop always thinking with your earthly mind, and allow your heavenly spirit to guide you. Stop looking outward for comfort. People expend too much energy looking for worldly comforts, looking for the approval of society, looking for approval from the people around you.

You don't need others approval, you don't need others advice, everyone is searching for approval from the small circle they move in. Approval from your heavenly Father is all you ever need. Pray to your Father who is just waiting for you to talk to Him.

More important you must turn away from the media driven, false uninspiring secular world you inhabit, stop looking outwardly for lasting happiness in this life, there is none, stop looking outwardly for lasting beauty in this life, there is none.

Concentrate on your journey to the next world, the place you are destined to live for eternity. If you only look, this eternal world of the spirit is already with you. It is there deep in your inner being.

The perfect peace that everyone is searching for is within them. Look inwardly to the lasting happiness of the soul, look inward to the lasting beauty of the spirit, these are perfections within, these are the only important elements of your being that matter.

This is what justifies your existence. Prayer will awaken you to this.

Some days I feel great and then other days I feel very depressed. What causes this?

Some days you experience a feeling of elation, a great feeling of well-being, a feeling that all is well in the world, and you wonder how you are feeling so good on this particular day, this feeling in fact is a surge of the soul.
It comes from a welling up of hope in the soul, all hope comes from the soul. All feelings of happiness and well-being come from within your soul.

Prayer will awaken you to this: lasting beauty of the spirit

When you are feeling depressed it always means that the evil spirit is making a surge to depress your spiritually, in times like this you must pray harder and more often. Do not let it get the better of you.

If you are seeking perfections in this world, then look again, there are none. Your whole life is a journey to perfection. There is no such thing as perfection of the flesh, the only perfection you can ever achieve is perfection of the soul. Perfections are attributes of God, not of man.

If you look to Him for comfort, you will find it, and if you look to Him for acceptance of your imperfections, you will find peace. This is as much as you can have in this life, peace. You will never find lasting happiness.

Can we not overcome our imperfections, our shortcomings, our failings, and aim for to achieve perfection?

The main lesson in this life is to learn how to accept your human failings, your human shortcomings, your imperfections. You will never overcome them, you must just learn how to deal with them. The human element will never take you to where you want to go.

It can never give you what the human heart yearns for. All achievement in this life is hollow, because it is short lived.

Humans are imperfect. Stop looking to heal your imperfections in this life, you never will. You must accept them and learn to deal with them. Human beings are imperfect because they are born of other humans that are also imperfect.

That is the way you were born. You inherited these imperfections. Stop blaming yourself for them. If you were born with a physical deformity you wouldn't blame yourself. So stop blaming yourself for emotional deformities you are born with. To deal with these is the trial, called life.

I have heard from another religion that they believe that if you have no commitment to anything outside this life, then when you die your body and soul stays in this life?

Your soul will never stay in this life. It either ascends or descends when you die which will all be decided for you on Judgement Day.

How can we find our way in this morass of confusion in the world today?

Always let the Lord show you the way, let Him lead you in truth and happiness. If you do, wonderful things will happen. Do not limit God ever. He cares and provides for everything in this world. It is man that corrupts His gifts and spits on them.

In allowing God to act you must resist self, or planning your own life without including Him. Do not plan your own way ahead. Without God in your plan, life will become very complicated.

But it is fear of tomorrow that makes us want to plan ahead ourselves, tomorrow is always a worry to humans.

Leave tomorrow's worry to God. Christ is a great eliminator of worry, so what you do with a worry for tomorrow is hand it over in prayer to Jesus before you go to bed, tell Jesus you are letting Him deal with it.

And you will be amazed, it may not happen immediately the next morning but before very long, there will be an extraordinary change in the problem you thought you had from the previous day. Keep nothing back from God, tell Him all and wait for Him to act.

But what about Satan and evil, he always rears his ugly head, no matter how you try to avoid him?

Jesus said, love Me and do My will, and no evil will befall you. Do not worry about evil that you might encounter. Just put your trust in God. He will counter any evil that befalls you. His presence in your life protects you and will bring you the peace you crave for.

Always let the Lord show you the way, let Him lead you in truth and happiness.

All requests of Jesus brings fulfilment, and in a way you may never expect. If you put your life in His Hands your life will flow peacefully, like a tranquil river.

But sometimes continuous prayer seems pointless, why should we pray every day when we may not have anything specific to pray for?

You must always continue your prayers, even if sometimes it seems fruitless not to be praying for a specific need. Satan will try by any means to disrupt your time set aside for prayer.

Never neglect times for prayer, pray and read your Bible, discipline yourself to set time aside for prayer every day. Always pray before you go to sleep at night, and when you wake in the morning.

God expects you to pray continuously, do not worry about directing that prayer towards a specific need, God knows where to direct your prayer, and it is all beneficial to you and your family, both living and dead.

To offer prayer in thanksgiving to God must be a continuous commitment in your life, to use those prayers where you and your family need them, is God's continuous commitment to you.

How does God use these prayers?

When you pray, even though your prayer is not said for any named reason, these prayers will open the way for souls in need, especially in your family. God uses all prayers and directs them where they are most needed, and His plans for the use of these prayers may be immediate or may just unfold in time.

Is it only on receipt of prayers that God acts?

Prayer is the Key, and no door is too difficult for God to open with this key.

Have other people's prayers benefited me?

You may be sure other people's prayers have benefited you in the past. Many of the good things that have happened in your life have been the result of someone elses prayers. You should not forget all the graces you have received through others prayers.

Through prayer, every fleeting thought may be answered, every wish gratified, every deed achieved. O if the world only realised how near God is, and how powerful prayer is, there would not be as much needless suffering in the world.

But I have said a prayer from time to time that I don't think was answered?

But remember you must wait for prayer to work, miracles do not happen in the moment you say the prayer, as men often expect, they happen in God's time, if it is right for your soul, and your future well-being.

The apostle Peter was not changed overnight from a simple, uneducated and rough boisterous fisherman into a great apostle, he was allowed time for denial.

He was allowed time to pray to overcome his weakness first. Peter could never have been the power in the world he was, had he not first understood his weaknesses.

The call comes some day for all men to follow Jesus, to rise up from their earthbound foolishness, from sin, depression, distrust, fear, and all that hinders your life's journey towards eternity.

So escape from your journey to everlasting death, and work towards your journey to everlasting life, by overcoming all your weaknesses.

Remember that death is the enemy you must destroy. Jesus gives you the chance to destroy it, He gives you the chance of life instead of death.

All sin is conquered through prayer, pray every day as you live, as you move about, and as you work. Prayer defeats all that depresses you, all that you fear in this life will be powerless through prayer.

So let nothing hinder you from attaining your risen life. Rise with Christ, to eternity. Let your voice in the Heavens be heard to say some day **"I live"**.

Miracles do happen in God's time, if it is right for your soul and your future well-being.

Is man not just another living creature, like any other animal on this earth?

Your existence is part of the pattern and plan of all nature, but that plan was laid out by divine providence. And the most important thing to remember is that in that plan, man is the only living creature that has been given the gift of choice and free will.

But if my life is part of a large plan created by divine providence, then how can I have free will? And if I have free will then Divine Providence can not influence choices in my life, surely it must be one or the other.

The daily experiences of all living creatures must show them that there are many signs in peoples daily lives that prove the influence of Divine Providence in the form of guidance. If you had not this influence then your life would be chaotic.

What are these signs?

Well the most common would be in the form of enlightened thought, influenced by your conscience to guide your decisions in life. And there is ongoing last second physical restraint to influence avoidance of what could have been a tragic event in your life, this should prove to people that Divine Providence is continuously active in their everyday life.

And this activity is to keep your earthly life intact, so that you are free to have the time to exercise your free will in matters of the soul. But you know you are free to make use of your own will and wisdom when making everyday choices in matters of the soul. The evidence is all around you, but you have to look at it, if you are too dismissive of it or choose to ignore it, then you may miss it altogether.

And of course, this freedom to choose can lead you into sin, but you will always hear an inner warning voice, which is your conscience, and when you deliberately ignore it, then that is the exercise of your free will.

Will this world ever end and if so when will it end?

Yes of course, the world will end, it ends for everyone, but I can only tell you when the world will end for you, but you are not ready for that information yet.

But why can't you tell me now?

Because you are not ready to know this now, you have many more important questions within you that you need answers to, and when I have answered these questions, you will understand a lot more and then your soul will be prepared, then I can tell you about the end of the world.

When I think you are ready for this answer I will tell you.

Is the Catholic religion the one true religion?

The Catholic religion is the one true religion for you, and will truly save you if you adhere to its teaching.

That's not exactly answering my question.

Well let me put it this way, everything you have learned in your religious teaching is correct and true.

Everything you have learned about God in your Catholic up-bringing is true in every way, and no other religious teaching is of any benefit as far as faith in God is concerned, and as far as your salvation is concerned.

If you followed the catholic religious teaching you received in your young life, your entry into the next life would be guaranteed.

What I can also confirm is that all the ritual, as you call it, that you have adhered to in your Catholic life contributes in a considerable way towards the salvation of your soul.

Are you saying that everything that I did as a youth that I consider today was just Catholic ritual and ceremony, was important to my soul, such as when I was an altar boy or choirboy?

Let me ask you this, did you feel good when you performed as an altar boy and choirboy all those years ago?

Yes come to think of it I felt very good and very important, but that was just boyishness, feeling like somebody important for the first time, wasn't it?

John, when you became an altar boy, you were somebody important for the first time. What you felt then, John, was happiness of the soul, the only real fulfilling happiness in this life, the happiness obtained in serving God sincerely, as you did then.

The happiness of the soul, the only real fulfilling happiness in this life is the happiness obtained in serving God sincerely.

And anything you did then that helped others to practice their belief and worship of God was not only important to you then, but also important to you now.

You can change your mind about what you believed in the past but you cannot negate it, it is there forever registered on your soul, and it contributes to me being able to be here now, and to my easing your path into the next life.

And what about the ritual of going to confession even when I didn't have any real sins to tell the priest, all the times I went to confession as a youth when I didn't even know what a serious sin was, are you saying that is also a help to me now?

What you had then will never leave you, even though you may think it has, it is ingrained deep within your being, it was part of you then and is still part of you now.

You may keep it hidden and dormant, but it is there like a bank account, if you make a lodgement it will always be there to your credit.

It was important to your development and is part of your life and the reason why I am able to come to you now, to help save your soul.

I don't understand still why this was necessary?

When you see animals like lion cubs horseplay around with each other shortly after they are born it has a lot more importance that it seems, it is a vital part of nature's way of preparation for their development and their way of life.

What you learn or take in at a young age stays with you for the rest of your life and if you disregard it in later life it always leaves a void that you will never fill.

It is belief in God that makes you more than just another species of animal.

Is there a basic rule that will lead man to eternal life?

If you asked me to describe the way to eternal life in one word, that word would be sincerity.

If you are sincere in everything you do in life, you can't go far wrong. Your salvation comes from your sincerity in the way you live your life.

Your sincerity in trying to live your life the way you believe God wishes you to live it. Your sincerity in your relationships with other people. Your sincerity in your search to know God.

The opposite to this of course is insincerity, which

brings us to one word which will ensure you won't reach eternal life, and that word is malice.

You should never have malice in your life, especially in your dealings with other people, because this is the greatest of all evils.

If you are sincere without any malice in you, then you will have love. Love for everything that God has created. That includes the earth itself, as well as all life he has put on it, because this earth and all on this earth, belongs to the creator, which is God.

How should we pray?

You should pray to be a Christian in the real sense of the word, that is a follower of Christ's teaching. You should pray for personal understanding of what God expects from you, and remember, for you, that may be different from anyone else.

Everyone in this world has to live a different life, no two people are the same, so what God expects from you, may not be the same as he expects from your brother or sister. The mistake that people sometimes make is comparing themselves with other people, or trying to model their life on someone else's.

Your role in God's plan may be a lot different to theirs. You, for some reason may not be given the grace to do what they were given the grace to do. All you need to achieve in life is that which God has given you the ability to achieve.

He will never give you the grace to achieve that which He hasn't asked of you.

The second mistake you can make is to compare other people to yourself, expecting them to live their life to your expectations. You cannot do this; they will only have the ability and the grace to do what God expects of them in this life.

Nature is part of God's plan, and nature allows random genes from your family line to combine, so that each person is therefore unique.

This means that you may have in your bank of genes, a combination that come from many different people in your family lineage going back through the whole history of time.

Therefore every person born is born with a different mix of genes, making them a unique individual with different physical and mental faculties to anyone else. So God may expect something completely different from you, than from any other person.

Because your life is governed by the genes that combined to make you. And this is why you always should pray to know what God expects from you. And pray for enlightenment in your search for your road to eternal life.

You pray for help to live your life as a follower of Christ. And because your faculties may be different, you pray never to do anyone any harm either by design or inadvertently, in your efforts to save your own soul.

This is why you always should pray to know what God expects from you

Can your spirit and your body be going in different directions, can your body sometimes act of its own will and go against your spirit?

You are not two people, you are only one person, your spirit is you, your body is only a flesh encasement around the spirit. Your mind is your spirit, your soul is your spirit.

Your spirit is not something inside you, like a spirit person, inside a body person. When you talk to yourself you are talking to your spirit.

On judgement day the spirit can't expect to go into eternal life by claiming it had nothing to do with the flesh. On earth your spirit and your flesh are one and the same, but only one.

What about my brain, is it not independent of everything else?

Every part of your body is ancillary to the spirit, your bones are reinforcement for the flesh and your tissue and blood, heart and organs are to give your body mobility and longevity. Your brain is just an analytical guidance instrument.

The body decides nothing for itself, it only does what the spirit tells it. If you are not looking after your spirit you are not looking after your body.

If you weaken the spirit you also weaken the body. Only the body feels pain, which is a warning to show you that you are neglecting the spirit.

In any situation where your body suffers, look into your soul and you will find the answer there.

You see, people don't seem to understand that your physical health is entirely dependent on your spiritual health, if your spiritual state of mind is balanced and in conformity, then so too will your body health be balanced and in conformity.

Your mind is your spiritual control tower; it controls every thing coming into your head and into your body.

If you just take in healthy things into your being, you will have a healthy mind and a healthy body. When your body finally dies your spirit passes into another dimension.

This is why if you reach the next life, eternal life, there is no pain and no suffering, because you leave your body behind, and only the body feels pain, the spirit cannot feel pain.

Are you saying the spirit can never feel pain?

Your spirit cannot feel physical or mental pain because

it is a perfect spiritual entity. There is no suffering of any kind in the spirit only dimension.

What do you think of people's beliefs today?

I think a lot of people are misled in their beliefs today. They hear a so-called new visionary, who conveys the meandering of his or her mind as a window into the spirit world, believing them to be mystical insights. This is diverting souls.

They believe that every new book they come across, published by some obscure author about new ways to come to God, has been given to them by providence. This is diverting souls.

You would learn much more about your God by going into a quiet church and contemplating Him there, talking to Him quietly about all your fears, handing Him all your troubles. Asking Him for understanding of your problems and your life.

Eternal life comes from talking and listening to God, through prayer and reading the Bible, in the Holy Mass, and in the confessional.

He is there waiting for you in the Church He founded, go there in your search for salvation.

Eternal life comes from talking and listening to God, through prayer and reading the Bible, in the Holy Mass, and in the confessional.

We are today supposed to live in a civilized world, yet there is still so much hatred in the world, so many people opposed to each other?

There are no differences in people, all people are the same by nature, but there are vast differences in people's thinking because of different influences, indifferent environments, and different cultures.

But all human differences whether man admits to it or not, are ultimately religious ones.

For instance no man ever born has not pondered the question of how he and the world that he lives in began?

The question of why intelligent life, which is man, is separated from all other forms of life on this earth?

The question why he is the only life form that has been given a clear inherent understanding of what is good and what is evil?

Why has animal life not got a conscience and a soul?

And no man ever born has not given thought to the existence of God, resulting in him becoming part of some organised belief, which thereafter divides him from other men because of this difference in belief.

But what about great scientific men like Darwin who have claimed that the first life came about in the depths of the oceans and all life has evolved from the sea, and from that all life has developed through evolution to the level of intellectual man today?

Well, let's examine Darwin's claims, that intelligent life on earth is a process of evolution. And that human life began in the sea, eventually coming up onto dry land where legs and air breathing lungs evolved, then from this life evolved into upright creatures of which the so called primate was the first, then the final process of evolution from primate to man.

At what time in this evolution did this evolving creature get a soul and a conscience and emotional feelings, Darwin never explains this evolvement.

And if evolution is a natural process of nature then why has it not continued? According to Darwin it is a continuous process. Why then are there any fish left?

Why are there still monkeys in the trees? If his theory of continuous evolution was to stand up, why then hasn't all life evolved into man in the millions of years that have gone by since the beginning of the world?

Surely you must come to the conclusion that if his theory is correct, then this natural process of evolution at this stage in the earth's history should be complete, and there should be no fish left in the sea or monkeys left in the trees, there should only be man.

You know what cannot be disputed is that man with his simple basic knowledge of nature, and through simple deduction has in the past come much closer to the truth than all those educated intellectual minds trying to intellectualise life, and give a scientific explanation for everything.

Understanding nature and the evolution of man does not need a scientific revelation.

With all of today's involved theories, which just create confusion, doubts and uncertainty, intellectual and sophisticated man seems to know less about life since the loudly heralded scientific revolution than he ever did. Because he is looking in the wrong place.

The origin and end of mankind is much more fundamental than the confused complex view people try to put on it today. Even primitive man was much closer to the truth with his simple theory of life.

Another fundamental is that modern man with his mostly hedonistic attitude to life knows deep within that ultimately he has to justify his every thought and deed on this earth, and it is one of his deepest and most suppressed fears.

In all human life there is a definitive which is a fundamental to all human understanding, and which is inwardly visible to the very simplest or the most intellectual mind, and that is the clear line between right and wrong, the line between good and evil.

No human ever born to this earth is not acutely aware of this. And it is the basis on which all decisions should be made, whether it be a very simple matter, or a world defining one.

When a man commits a mortal offence against God's elemental laws, he knows it regardless of his politics, his religious beliefs, or cultural origin.

Another thing that is certain, is that the peace of mind on this earth that man so desperately seeks will never be advanced by scientific theories or philosophical thinking, his mind can only find peace by spiritual contemplation and communion with God.

Real evil began when men who were given special abilities and gifts in life, turned their back on their natural instincts of goodness instilled in them by God, and turned away from helping to feed the weak and vulnerable, in order to feed their own ambitions.

Is the person most pleasing to God then, one who is both religious and intellectual and therefore one who is both in a position and willing to help the poor, weak and vulnerable?

Great spirituality and great intellectual minds are a wondrous combination, but seldom found in the same person. The type of person most pleasing to God is the person that is saddened not by their own problems, but by the problems of others. God's greatest joy is when he sees a man who has little in the world, giving help to the person who has less.

Or when he hears one of His creation praying for another soul that needs His help.

In other words God loves those who love their neighbour and who trust in God so much that they never pray for themselves but always offer up their prayers for those less fortunate than themselves.

God has very little time for selfish people who spend their prayer life praying for themselves and their own wants endlessly, there is a lack of understanding of God's nature in these people.

But surely if you have a need, then you are entitled to pray for your own needs and to ask God's help for yourself.

Yes of course you are but what I am trying to emphasise is that God bestows more love on you when you pray for someone else than when you pray for yourself. This is what being a Christian is all about. A Christian should be Christ like;

Christ gave his whole life for others, which is why the Father had so much love for His Son.

God loves those who love their neighbour and who trust in God so much that they never pray for themselves but always offer up their prayers for those less fortunate than themselves.

Give me an example of someone who has lived this kind of life on earth besides Christ?

Well, in your lifetime you had Saint Maximillian Kolbe who was a great example of a Christ-like Christian. His own suffering although extreme was not something he ever gave a thought to, because he knew where he was going and that suffering on this earth is only short lived, and can be a means to saving other souls as well as your own.

This demonstrates to God the love of man for his fellow man, which is the way and the light that Christ demonstrated on the cross: the way to eternal life, is the way of unconditional love.

Maximillian Kolbe suffered like Christ for someone he did not even know, but looking through Christ's eyes at his neighbour, his fellow man, he saw someone who was suffering because of his paternal love for his family.

So Maximillian Kolbe offered his body up to terrible suffering ending in death, in order to save his fellow man, his neighbour from this terrible fate.

Christ took on the suffering that justice demanded and should have been meted out to mankind, He did this in order to save the death of mankind's soul, and give it another chance to be reconciled with the Father in heaven.

Many more women seem to attend the sacraments than men, can I ask you are women closer to God than men?

No, you cannot say anything definitive like that in assessing a religious difference in the genders, but you could say that there are many more women close to God than men, and in much greater numbers.

Many more women attend the sacraments, and their prayers and continuing respect for the Church stays the hand of justice in many situations that could be disastrously different. It is the mothers of the world that have kept the Catholic Church alive.

Are women then more practical as well as more religious than men?

Well, I would have to answer you in a similar way: you cannot say anything definitive like that, but I could qualify the answer by saying that many women are more religious as well as more practical than their male counterparts in many walks of life.

But still it is men that have become the great leaders of the Church, and the greatest Saints of the Church, is that not so?

But you will find in many cases that it was a pious mother that reared and guided these men, it was the influence of their mothers that brought them to this holiness in the first place. And down through the history of the Church it was the influence of mothers on the sons that prospered the faith especially in difficult times for the church.

The most important thing in life is to reconcile one's soul with the Lord, if you fall into sin.

Are there therefore many more male sinners in the world than female?

Yes that is right, and I suppose the reason for this is that men, not being so confined to the home and not having to look after the children and family affairs, are more open to the occasion of sin.

And therefore fall more often, but worse is that most of them do not do as women do, go often to the Lord for reconciliation, and that is the real disaster.

Is all of this happening because of the modern world and the way we live life today?

No you can't say that, this has always been the way of the world, maybe even more so in the past than today.

Why then had the Lord no Women Apostles?

In the time of Our Lord in the world, women were even more confined to the home, and men had much more freedom to move about and much more authority to speak in the market place. When Christ came to earth He had to accept the world as it was then.

Women held a very lowly place in society. They were uneducated and were restricted to the home, if Jesus had chosen them as His speakers in the market place they would have been scorned or ignored, and maybe even abused.

He had the greatest respect and sympathy for women, but He had to do the work He was sent to do in the best way possible, under the circumstances that existed in society at that time, with the best results in mind.

He therefore chose sincere men from different walks of life that he knew would be able to get their fellow men to listen to them. Men that would give their lives to spread the message of the Good News.

My father had a devotion to the Sacred Heart only. He had no devotion to any Saint or even Our Lady, I would often hear him say "I talk to the top man only". My mother always said it was just as important to have devotion to Our Lady as well as Our Lord. Was my father in error?

Your father was like a lot of men of his age, it was a kind of male thing with a lot of them. Of course it would have been great for your father if he had a balanced attitude, but he was at the feet of the Sacred Heart when he prayed, and that would be all that Our Lady would have wanted from him, to come to the feet of her son and worship.

I remember having a discussion with a man who believed in nothing and his question was who is this God? What does he do? He said, I never meet him, I never see him, who is he? What does he do?
How could I answer him? What should I have said?

Well you could have said, next time the sun shines on you look to one side and you will see a shadow, that is from God, if you have no shadow then God doesn't exist, and neither do you.

God is the reason we exist, He is the ability to exist. But after you are created, you are given the choice to exist on the side of good, or you can exist on the side of evil. That is your only choice.

People say you cannot really enjoy this life without plenty of money, what do you say to that?

Enjoying life is being at peace with yourself, and at peace with your neighbour. It has nothing to do with having money, either a lot or very little.

You can enjoy life in both these situations if you are at peace. And being at peace means having God in your life. Do not let sin separate you from this peace.

Sins of human weakness are sins that God understands, remember God came to earth to make His mercy available to sinners, if you sin through

God is the reason we exist,

He is the ability to exist

human weakness then go to confession and God will renew you.

Today many people get married outside of church and they would claim that after all marriage is only a contract between two people to live together?

Remember, Marriage is a Sacrament and God created the Sacrament of Marriage; if you get married in a church then your contract is with God as well as with your spouse. If you do not get married in a church then you have no contract with God, and God is not part of your marriage.

No-one has confidence in priests any more because there has been so much bad news about them, they were once seen as special people, but not any more; can the priesthood survive, can the church survive?

Priests are men who have given their lives to the service of God, and to the service of the people. This is a huge sacrifice for any man to begin with, and many young men don't understand how much of a sacrifice this is, until well into their priesthood.

The pressures on their lives to become the perfect priest is enormous, and of course to achieve this they must become the perfect person. The pressure to remain the perfect person as a priest is about ten times more difficult than that of a lay person.

Yet many achieve this and become close to saints in their lives. Many people would know them, but the world of unbelievers does not want to know them.

The media does not want to know them, because that would not be sensational news. What the media want is to sell newspapers, and the certain way to do this is to report the people who fall from their pedestal, not the ones who stand tall upon it.

And it is only the evil in people that the media feed with this sadness, but unfortunately there is a lot of evil in the world. These people would not buy a paper if it was full of stories about holy people or saintly priests.

And if the truth was known there are many more good priests than there are bad ones. And this is the balance in all of society, if you analyse society there are many more good people than there are bad people. Otherwise the world would not survive.

God might not allow it to continue. God made a covenant with man, which man threw back in His face, then justice was done. God made a second covenant with man but this second covenant will be the last.

What type of signs do we get from God?

Sometimes you will hear an inner voice, it may be only a word but you should listen to it, it may be something you have never thought about much, because your subconscious tells you it is outside your realm of understanding.

But the word may be from your angel and it may be something you have to think about, because it is within your realm of responsibility and you may be expected to do something about it.

I often wake up at night. I seem to be woken by some noise that does not occur again as I lie there listening to hear it again, what is that?

You may be awakened by a distinct sound in the early hours of the morning, you wait to hear it again but it doesn't happen again, but you know the sound was quite clear that woke you.

That sound may be a sign that someone wants to communicate with you, it may be from someone seeking your help in prayer, you should pray at that time for who ever comes to mind, that has left this life.

If you are unsure, pray and ask God to accept your prayer for the person seeking it.

What happens to poor children that are aborted, are these souls lost for all time?

In a way incomprehensible to human minds, all souls are encompassed in God's salvific plan. In a way that only God knows, all souls are given the chance to accept or reject God's grace, and thereby earn themselves a place in heaven.

This extends to the unborn, the mentally handicapped of whatever age, and children that die in whatever circumstances, before the age of reason. All humans without the gift of reasoning are incapable of committing sin, and therefore cannot be punished by never seeing God.

Humanity at any age cannot lose its soul inadvertently, but only when they have the opportunity of rejecting God.

You may never understand this. This is God's way, and many of His ways will never be understood by man. Remember, God is always just and merciful and has unconditional love for all of His creation.

Why is it important for a priest or religious to be celibate?

Because Christ calls certain people to follow Him, and this means to live a life similar to His, in order to be pure in preaching the Gospel and be free of any other influences that might affect their dedication to the service of His word.

Pure meaning pure in thought, and interpretation of the Gospel, which only those who have given their lives totally and unconditionally to Christ, will understand.

Christ's great sacrifice on the Cross was to demonstrate to the Father His love for all humanity and to beg mercy on the sins of the world. This was the act that won redemption for mankind, which was Christ's great gift to the world.

Therefore those who answer His call are choosing to give their life to Him in representing Him on Earth and their sacrifice demonstrates to the Father their love for Christ and their fellow man, and their hope that this sacrifice like Christ's, will be accepted by the Father, on behalf of all they serve.

Remember, this gift to the Father if they maintain their celibacy makes them very privileged people and places them in a powerful position to appeal to the Father for graces for the souls they serve.

A celibate priest's prayer becomes inseparable from the prayer and sacrifice of Christ.

Can people atone for other people's sins and be saved from purgatory by others prayers?

On earth serious or continuous sin loses you the protection of your Guardian angel, and until you repent, get absolution and are purified and reconciled with God, your angel will not return, and you are always in danger of losing your eternal life if you die in that state.

If you die in a state of sin but not serious sin then you go to Purgatory where you still have a chance of being purified by others prayers, and those who offer sacrifice or Holy Masses in atonement for your sins.

I hear of people being called by God, how does this happen?

A call from God can come by means of your guardian angel, by hearing a heavenly voice, or by an unusual happening in your life which changes it, and these people will always recognise that they have had a calling from God.

This is known as a spiritual calling. It is an appeal from God to do some special work for him, which sends the person that received it on a new journey in their life.

Like the children of Fatima who got their calling through an angel, there are thousands of privileged people who have got this special grace down through history.

Each person's call will be uniquely different, because each person is uniquely different. Their backgrounds, their personalities, their culture and the time in which they live.

From then on, Divine Providence will be seen to act frequently in their lives. This call is heard within the dimensions of one's inner being and people are changed completely as a result, their lives become inseparable from the experience of that call and their new relationship with God.

They never see God in the same way thereafter.

Who are the people God calls, are they people he knows are of good faith, or have a great ability to speak or to write on Gospel? What do they have that other less privileged people don't have?

When God calls someone, He does not single them out for their particular abilities. He does not choose people who are well known or have special talents, in fact He always seems to pick those who have no special talent or qualities.

It is usually people that are very simple and uncomplicated, often uneducated and sometimes not even renowned for being overly religious.

The reason God picks these people is because He wants people to see and hear something unique and profound coming from this person and that it will be evident that the message must be coming from another source, and that therefore it is not coming from that person but comes through them.

God normally only calls individuals when he has a message for mankind.

Are intellectual people and people with wealth much further away from God, because of their exceptional position?

No, whatever your situation is in life, it is about surrendering yourself to God in whatever your standing is in life.

That means not being preoccupied with your material wealth or your exceptional intellect, it means having God in all your decisions, and always being moral and doing things after you have consulted an informed conscience.

The secret of life is to be guided always by love, love of God which influences all things good, and love of your fellow man which inspires reciprocal love in all humanity.

Aggression and hate can inspire the same in return, love always inspires love in return.

It is very hard for a man not to respond to aggression whether it be physical or verbal, surely this is part of his manly nature?

If someone seeks physical confrontation, Jesus preached to turn the other cheek and walk away from it, if someone calls you names, you should not respond, but just walk away, do not get involved in a verbal confrontation.

In both cases it reflects your Christian belief.

The secret of life is to be guided always by love, love of God which influences all things good.

But what if they are in the wrong should you not respond, like when they give false witness against you?

If a person gives false witness, then let the Lord deal with it, you can be sure God will not deal lightly with people who get involved with false testimony against others.

This is one of the most serious offences in God's eyes. If it is deliberate false testimony, it is a serious mortal sin, and as a consequence they will suffer greatly, both in this life, as well as in the next.

I hear visionaries today prophesising the future, is there such a thing as someone being able to prophesise the future, many people scoff at prophets today and the media have no belief in this phenomena at all, and just make fun of visionaries and prophets?

If you read the history of the Church you will see that St. Paul welcomed prophecy as a great gift to the church, because the prophet's appearance within a community indicated that the Spirit was alive in the midst of that community.

However, the prophets even in his time did not always receive enthusiastic welcomes.

Many faced jeers and stoning, while still others were

chained and put in prison. They were some who were flogged and even put to death by the sword.

They went about in sheepskins and goatskins, destitute, persecuted, and mistreated in the world of their time.

People who do not want the world to believe in God would not want anyone to believe in prophets, because that would be evidence of the Holy Spirit in the world, which would mean that they are not masters of their own destiny.

A lot of people think that you must give up everything to follow Jesus. Does Jesus expect people to renounce everything in order to follow Him?

No, such a practice would be socially and economically unworkable. If that was the case who would be left to support the poor and thereby to fulfil the Lord's commands about feeding the hungry and clothing the naked?

The solution is to use one's wealth as if you do not own it, realising all wealth comes from God.

The poverty that God speaks about touches every human being, whether or not you enjoy material prosperity or not, because it is the poverty of the human spirit that can affect all souls.

You can be rich and still live according to the faith. But where there is material poverty a burden rests across the shoulders of those who have both material wealth and faith, and that responsibility flogging on society will always be there.

The way to measure the sincerity of people's efforts to deal with material poverty is to look at the efforts they make to seek awareness of the living conditions of others, the hunger, the injustice, the powerlessness and deprivation, which much of the world endures.

You must see the poor wherever they are as your sisters and brothers and understand that the poor in God's eyes belong to all Christians. Your salvation depends on this.

Catholics should remember that all the faithful of Christ of whatever rank or status are called to the fullness of the Christian life and to the perfection of charity, this is real holiness which is cultivated by all who are moved by the Spirit of God.

No Catholic can call themselves real Christians and claim to live out the gospel wholeheartedly, if they do not pledge themselves to selfless love of the poor, and thereby fulfil God's command to feed the hungry and clothe the naked.

How is it that men and women seem to have completely different views on how to bring up children? They say today that a child is better off with only one parent. Would children be better off with only one parent?

To mature into complete balanced adults, children need love from two parents. Parental love is of two different kinds, unconditional and conditional.

The mother's love is unconditional, the father's is conditional. The child needs both.

A mother loves her children because they are her children, and for no other reason. She loves them whether they accomplish much or little.

In fact, she loves them no matter what they do, for better or worse. The mother of a serial killer will still love her child even though she despises his deeds. This is her maternal biology, that is the female nature.

Man's nature is to teach his child independence. Like the hunter has to teach his progeny how to survive by making sure they learn how to hunt for themselves.

So he needs to see his child accomplish for themselves, otherwise his biology or nature tells him he has failed in his duty. A man has an inbuilt fear of his child being vulnerable in a hostile world.

When people say they have found God do you mean the Catholic religion?

People do not always find God through the Catholic religion, to find God through any religion that leads you to God is good. You cannot depreciate any religion, all of mankind belongs to God, all men were created equal by God and they all had the same religion when created, thereafter it was human minds that created divisions and different religions.

Different religions are only different ways of searching for God, not for different Gods because this would be impossible, because there is only one God.

Remember Christ died for all mankind which includes those of all religions and even those of none.

Then what is the difference in Religions? Religion seems to be the cause of a lot of suffering and wars in the world.

In this life all people cause suffering to others. Jews cause suffering, Christians cause suffering, Muslims cause suffering, Hindus cause suffering, Buddhists cause suffering.

But all religions are on an affirmative path, They all affirm the existence of a supreme being, or God, a God who you must commune with, to help you in your life.

This communion is achieved by reaching out to God through prayer, through study of Scripture, through observance of religious ritual, which is showing respect and giving witness to your belief in God.

Those who believe in God show it through leading a good life, and having respect and tolerance for others beliefs and way of life.

This belief is also demonstrated by offering comfort and help to those who are suffering in this world. Judaism, Christianity, Islam, Hinduism and Buddhism and many other religions, they all believe in a promise that by living a good life and helping others results in a reward of eternal life.

All the people in this world want to believe in a supreme being. But all too often those searching for God, are misled by corrupt people who claim to be God's representatives, with corrupt doctrines.

If anyone teaches hatred and violence and intolerance, you may be sure that they are not helping people find God.

All of these religions I mention have doctrines of peace. If anyone teaches that some humans are less than other humans, calling them demons, or infidels, then they are not part of any of these religions and are definitely not leading their followers to eternal life.

How can peoples beliefs and actions vary so much if it is the same God?

Because you are talking about humans, creatures who God has given free will.

The extraordinary thing about human free will and human temperament is that not only do religious beliefs differ, but no matter what anyone comes to believe about anything, you will always find someone who believes the opposite, or something that will be completely incompatible with the first belief.

This can lead to human actions that are contradictory or incompatible. Christians are not excluded from this.

The pagan Roman emperors cruelly put people to death for believing in Christianity. Some centuries later, the Inquisition cruelly put people to death for not believing in Christianity.

I often wondered what exactly is the spark of life? What is the force that makes all of the elements that make the body work? Is it our spirit that sparks and ignites our movements and where in the body is the spirit, where does the ignition come from?

The spark or life force as you call it, comes from God and it is not part of the body. A human being is made up of two parts, flesh, bone, blood, and chemicals is the first or "human" part and the "being" is the second part. Or put it another way, the human is matter and form. When man is alive he is a human being but when he is dead he is still a human but not a "being" any longer.

How can I explain it so that you will understand? Some time ago there was a scientific study that came to certain conclusions.

Think of it this way, just say you are completely still and you just think to yourself " I will move my big toe" you can do this without moving any other part of your body.

Your big toe moves, but what caused your big toe to move was an impulse from the brain, that impulse activated a nerve down through your spinal cord, then down through your leg, across your foot and activated the muscle which moves your big toe. And it all happens instantly at the speed of light.

You will not understand this, but the thought or the wish to move your big toe that created the impulse comes from outside the body.

Scientists through scientific studies could show how the impulse activated the nervous system and how the nervous system in conjunction with the chemicals in the body activates all the working parts.

The only thing they could not understand was how and where the thought to start the impulse formed and where it came from, because this cannot be explained by science because this is in the realm of the spiritual.

The spark, the life force, is the thought, which does not come from within the body, but the body is needed to put form on the thought. Without thoughts to create the impulse in the first place to activate the nervous system, the body would be paralysed.

When you're dead the human part is no longer active, but your being is still active, only then it is a "spirit being" not a "human being"

The problem with science is that scientists do not report on something they do not understand, what they do not understand is left unsaid, they cannot deal with the spiritual which is God.

How would you know a good priest today, it is only after a public disclosure that we realise that a particular priest is bad and then we know he was not sincere about his vocation.

A good priest today will inspire you when you hear him speak, especially by his homily. He will always speak about the coming of the Lord, and the Holy Spirit will speak through him, and you will be lifted up by his words and get a feeling of well being, and from the altar he will only speak on the Gospel, all Mass homilies should be taken from or inspired by the Gospels.

A good priest today will inspire you when you hear him speak.

What books should I read that will help me to believe in God and eventually lead me to Heaven?

No book and no person alone will help you believe in God or lead you to Heaven. Other people may help you to understand aspects of faith in God which you don't understand, but the search must be yours and ultimately the belief must be yours.

You must through your own efforts find God and through contemplation and prayer find true belief in Him.

When you pray, ask God to enlighten you, to give you real belief to give you real conviction. Do not be happy just with a routine of prescribed prayers.

Talk directly to God from your heart with your own words. Use words that you would use talking to a friend or your own mother, or father.

But don't always use prescribed prayers to commune with God, talk to the Father through Jesus and His Holy Spirit, He is the only guide or mediator you need to talk to the Father.

When you do this for a while you will be surprised how good you will feel and you will be surprised how God responds, if you talk to Him through Jesus.

You don't need to be led by other people to the Kingdom, you have to find and go there yourself. People have forgotten that the supreme mediator between God and man is Jesus Christ. Jesus is your Saviour and Jesus is your Redeemer.

When you enter the next life you will come face to face with your Saviour and only He can bring you into the Father's presence. The Father who is your creator is where all justice and mercy comes from.

Being a believer and follower of Christ takes effort, you have to work at it every day of your life. You cannot say you're a Christian by birth, or by tradition, or culture.

You cannot just choose to believe in God because of His promises, and the rewards to follow. The Devil believes in God, but he will never be a Christian.

You must have a conviction and that only comes through continuous effort and searching to understand your faith. You must engage personally in the search for the truth and convince yourself of it as far as you can.

It is between God and you. Directions from others you can take, but not their conclusions, the conclusions must be yours.

You can never adopt others understanding of God, you must find and understand God for yourself.

I have often heard of faithfulness being an important part of our religion, but doesn't this only apply to a married man? Who has a single man to be faithful to, if he is not married?

Faithfulness does not only apply to people in a marriage, it applies to all people in all circumstances in life. The most important virtue in life is integrity, and faithfulness is integrity.

This means that in life and in all circumstances you are the same person, not one person in one situation, and a different one in another, not projecting one image to one person and a different one to another.

The most important thing in your life is to be faithful to yourself. Faithfulness to God is also part of this, you must control your passions, this is what makes you a man in God's eyes.

What do you mean by passions?

There are many passions you have to control in yourself but anger is the worst passion, it leads to bad decisions made in haste.

It leads to hate, it leads to saying bad things about

another person, it leads in many instances to violence. It is only by controlling your passions that you can live in peace.

If you allow passion to take over your life you will always be a very unhappy person. The dignity of man requires him to control his passions with his mind, and not to allow his life to be led by thoughtless impulses.

It is said that it is a sin to be angry. But wasn't Jesus angry in the temple?

Anger was attributed to Jesus in the temple because of the similarity in effect of His extreme dissatisfaction with traders in the house of God.

He ejected them forcefully but that is not anger, that was being strong in determination to stamp out what was wrong. This was not the sin of anger.

Anger is when you lose control of your mind and your actions become irrational.

Sunday used to be a day when nobody worked but this has all changed, is it a mortal sin to work on Sunday, wasn't Jesus accused of working on Sunday?

If you read the Gospels it refers to Jesus being accused

of violating or working on the Sabbath. What Jesus said was that Sabbath was a day of holiness and that you must keep holy the Sabbath day, He said the Sabbath day was made for man, not man made for the Sabbath day.

Jesus declared this as a day for doing good. He said it is a day of mercy and a day to honour and praise God.

The Sabbath was a Jewish day of rest, but for Christians, Sunday, the day after the Sabbath, replaced it and is called the Lord's Day. On Sundays the faithful should not take part in anything that prevents them from the worship of their Creator.

You said to me that all thought comes from outside the body, but surely all thoughts comes from the brain?

The brain is a physical thing. The mind is not a physical thing. You can take an X ray of the brain but you cannot take an X ray of the mind, or of beliefs, conceptions, emotions, these things originate in the mind, and are only mirrored in the brain.

Your brain articulates your thoughts, that is its function. Your mind is something independent of the brain.

It is your will, your consciousness. When you lose consciousness your brain has to wait until your consciousness returns before it can articulate your thoughts again.

Minds are sources of consciousness. Thought is the radiance of the mind. Like a form of radiant energy, your mind is like a frequency, that the brain receptors pick up from your own individual frequency.

This radiant energy of the mind, is what you make judgements and decisions with, your brain articulates those judgements and decisions and then conveys them to the body.

Your consciousness is the source that allows you to

think. If you want to think clearly, you need to nourish your mind with the healthiest food available. That food is religious thought, as opposed to the myriad amounts of junk thought being published today.

Your life is a like a car. The engine makes the car go. If the engine is good and working then the car can take you places. But no matter how good the engine is, the car will go nowhere without a driver.

Your brain is the engine of your body. That driver is your consciousness, your mind. Without your mind your brain cannot function.

Has Divine Mercy always been there?

For man's full redemption, not only satisfaction was needed, grace had to be won for him, and this grace Christ won, on the cross.

Divine Mercy started when God created man. God's first act of Divine Mercy was in the beginning, when he created human beings out of nothingness, and then an environment for them to live in.

Then He showed His love by raising man to the level of sons and daughters of God and heirs to the Kingdom of Heaven.

Jesus   I Trust in   You

Divine Mercy started when God created man.

But when sin reduced mankind to nothingness again, then you see His greatest act of Divine Mercy, when as God-man He offered Himself up as a sacrifice through His Passion, Death and Resurrection and won the right from the Father to raise man up again from the depths of his misery, and fill him anew with hope of eternal life again.

His greatest Mercy was revealed at the Redemption, and by uniting in one Person the Divine nature and human nature, He became the Mediator between an offended God and sinful man.

He became a mediator, not in His divine nature but in His human nature, in union with the divine, for in His human nature He suffered and died, thus making infinite reparation.

What is our Cross in life?

Satan usually makes other people your Cross in life. Through other people you will be scourged on your way, you will be ridiculed, you will be made to suffer, you will be broken, and near to despair.

But true happiness only comes in the next life. If someone in this life is your Cross, just think maybe you are someone else's Cross as all mankind was Christ's Cross.

Why does God allow sin in the world?

You must be exposed to sin in order to reject it, that is the test. Like in the Garden of Eden, if Adam and Eve had no choice they could do no wrong.

A turnip in a field can do no wrong, but then Our Lord wanted man to be more than just a turnip. You cannot choose good without there being also a choice to choose evil.

What sort of mind is dangerous to your faith?

The most dangerous mind to encounter is a closed mind. One that is not prepared to listen to others who are going the same road searching for the same truth as they go.

You should never let other people choose your belief for you. Especially people who say they have all the answers. Those who tell you that, are those with closed minds themselves.

A closed mind is a mind that is afraid of facing up to the questions they may not easily find the answers to.

Everyone must face up to the difficult questions in life that challenge their faith. You must seek enlightenment and find answers to these questions by looking at others beliefs and with prayer and contemplation either take on board these theories or reject them.

But the answers will come in your search for the truth with the help of the Holy Spirit, He will strengthen your faith and allow you to defend it with conviction when you are challenged.

Hiding from reality and closing your mind is denying God the chance to enlighten you through prayer and reflection. To know God is to have a relationship directly with Him ourselves.

How does it happen that sometimes in life we suddenly feel very low, and nothing in particular brings it on?

Now, there are times when you have to accept the appearance of darkness in your life, and there are times when you are called to deal with this. Look at how often Jesus did. It will take shedding light on the darkness to dispel it.

All have to go through times when depression suddenly descends and an atmosphere of oppression overwhelms you, it is caused by demons, which seek only to disrupt your peace, and rob you of your joy which comes from goodness and closeness to God.

In some cases, the darkness may come from a certain

person, an area you go into, an object, or even your own home. It may come from what a person says to you, from a book, or a television programme, especially if these involve lewdness or the occult.

This force you must not allow to bring you down, you must defend yourself against it. You will receive grace from God for this; this is what God is pleased by. He may let you go right to the edge to see how you deal with evil.

The way to overcome evil is with good. You may not succeed by yourself but if you make the effort, God will rescue you.

 It may take a while to test your perseverance but He will pull you out of it and it will happen suddenly and as quickly as it descended (which is why you must always persevere, when evil attacks you).

The problem in bringing people to conversion is that you cannot prove there is a God.

Simple, intelligent reasoning should bring man to know there is a God, otherwise he is saying the universe is a place without meaning or purpose.

This would mean that the universe is an immense cosmic accident. And then it had to give birth to a myriad of sub-accidents to create the world that you know today.

This would mean that one of these accidents created the world, then a series of accidents happened in the world that created nature and all its wonder, another accident created the seasons and a specific order in the universe that was needed to keep the world going for thousands of years.

And finally the extraordinary accident that created man, in all his complexity. All of these accidents would mean that a series of events unfolded in the world over thousands of years without rhyme or reason.

And the spiritual therefore must be a figment of man's imagination. If the spiritual is a figment of man's imagination so too would be the moral essence of man, which means there is no such thing as good and evil, or any great struggle between good and evil.

Who or what then would define what is right and what is wrong, if man has no moral essence?

What is morality based on?

The very notion of morality involves a relationship with others. It also means thinking of others. Our responsibilities toward others arise from their very existence.

Concerns about one's own morality are not necessarily moral, for example just avoiding sin can be simply a matter of self-preservation. To be moral there is more than your own life involved.

You must have concern for your family, your neighbour, your community, and wherever there is a need that you can help.

Concern such as feeding the hungry, clothing the naked, helping the homeless, helping strangers, caring for the sick, and giving good example, that's all part of your morality.

Just helping yourself can have selfish or greedy connotations, which can even be immoral if you are in a position to help others, whereas helping others with something that they can not do for themselves always connotes a high moral act.

The whole conception of morality involves recognition of other people outside ourselves, as someone deserving of our assistance.

The human being must understand his or her full moral potential, through understanding that the very existence of other human beings, imposes inescapable moral obligations on them.

You must have an existential justification for a

universal ethic of caring. Your own happiness cannot be independent of others.

Are you talking about Christians helping other Christians, that is people of your own religion ?

When God replied to the question "who is my neighbour" in the Gospel, He did not limit your neighbour to your Christian neighbour, or your own ethnic group, He answered, "your neighbour is all mankind".

Today many Christians find it very hard to be moral, morality is for others not for them. They do not want to be kind to their neighbour.

They want to be free to do their own thing, free to indulge themselves at every opportunity.

And when the moral guardian of mankind, the Church, is scandalised by a number of it's servants who preach morals to others, but do not practice what they preach, they give an opportunity to those who wish to destroy the Church to get together and condemn the whole church.

How can I be a true Christian?

To be a true Christian you must never give in to despair, never allow yourself to descend to believing life is without meaning, you must always have hope in another life, otherwise this one has no meaning or purpose.

And always believe that Jesus can change any situation no matter how terrible. Also to be a true Christian you have to make hard choices, you should never make little of others especially those who have had no education or opportunity to improve their life.

You should be slow to criticise anyone, you should always turn the other cheek, this means when you are offended you must not react angrily, you must pray for those who persecute and calumniate you.

To be a true Christian you have to follow Christ, and you have to be prepared for sacrifices.

As a Christian your faith should not only be part of your everyday life, but your everyday life should be part of your faith.

Just remember that a Christian's life is the way of the Cross, that is what your life must be as a follower of Christ.

You must accept all that comes your way, all the suffering, all the hate, all that is thrown at you on your journey to your resurrection.

The end is the beginning. Only through death can you be resurrected into new life.

Like Christ, the way of your Cross is over only when you die.

Why have some people got a greater intellectual mind than other people, is this a gift of the spirit?

What is often referred to as 'gifted people' has nothing to do with the spirit, this is not a gift from God. These different exceptional intellectual or physical abilities that some people have and others haven't is part of the covenant of free will.

People are free to marry whomever they choose and from this marriage come a mixture of genes in all the progeny of these two people. So it is an accident of birth as to what gene mix you receive. So let me explain to you intellect, in the easiest way that I can.

Intellect is like athleticism of the brain, if the brain is exceptionally athletic and quick to learn and retain information, then it is exceptionally quick to access and analyse that information and arrive at answers.

But this is part of your body, not part of your spirit. It is like finding out you're a great athlete. You cannot choose to be a great athlete, it is firstly an accident of gene formation that gives you this special ability,

Remember that a Christian's life
is like the way of the Cross.

you then are in a position to develop this to greatness with training and practice.

But this has nothing to do with your spirit. Intellect is also an accident of gene formation, which you can also develop with education and knowledge.

But it also has nothing to do with your spirit. The spirit is the real you and in some cases you could be better off without these exceptional abilities.

Sometimes exceptional abilities can militate against the spirit and distract you from your real self, and you can even believe with this special ability that you are somehow in yourself special and above others because of this accident of gene formation.

You may even believe that you yourself created these abilities. You then think that the body is you, and you become completely blind to the spirit, and lose your way in the greater plan.

This is why Jesus had to come down and identify with man to bring light to his blindness and guide him on the way, and remind him to follow the spirit, not the body. *"I am the truth, the way and the light; to all who follow Me I will give eternal life"*.

The body is the human manifestation of the spirit on earth and it's purpose is to serve the spirit whilst on earth, but your body has a limited existence, your spirit is eternal.

Angels are spirits without a body; humans are spirits with a body. An angel is a spirit being, but you are a human being and a spirit being, until the human is no longer.

Is the human part of us animal?

You could say that, but the difference between humans and any other animal is that the human part may be animal but there is another part to you which is spiritual, and the spirit lives forever. And it is the human's spirit that makes man different from any other animal on earth.

Are you telling me that our bodies are the same as animals?

Well, you know that your spirit has a continuous battle to keep control of your body, because your body is animal by nature. It is always pulling against the spirit, it has urges that are completely against the spirit.

Has the body therefore animal instincts?

Yes, for instance the body always has aggressive urges just beneath the surface, ready to strike out at anything that aggravates it, that is the animal instinct.

It has a greed urge, which is contrary to the spirit, urges to possess what the other person has, like a wild animal after a kill has other animals coming around to try to take it from him.

The body has many evil urges that are animal instincts. All of these the spirit has to keep in check.

The Ten Commandments were given to you so that you would know what the spirit has to do to keep the body under control.

All the savagery that goes on in the world is committed by men who let their animal instincts take over and ignore their spirit, they are said to be men without a soul.

The body is the temple of your spirit on earth and has a purpose which is to serve the spirit whilst on earth.

The spirit should dominate the body but unfortunately on earth many people allow the body to dominate the spirit.

I am the Truth, the Way and the Light

"Help Us Dry The Tears"

("Divine Mercy in Action")

is a foundation started by
The Divine Mercy Apostolate in Dublin to help bring
the Mercy of God to the suffering street children of
Eastern Europe, Ecuador and Zambia, under the
Patronage of St. Joseph.

In honour of St. Joseph you may send
a donation to:

Bank Account No. 04975039
Branch No.93-22-48
Church Street Skerries,
Co. Dublin,
Ireland.

"Help Us Dry The Tears"
is a registered charity,
Charity No. CHY14320

If you wish a receipt please
forward your donation to
Divine Mercy Publications
Maryville, Skerries,
Co. Dublin, Ireland
Please Visit - www.hudt.org

All profits from
Divine Mercy Publications,
are donated to works of Mercy
with Street Children in Eastern Europe.

Since the collapse of the socialist system in Eastern Europe thousands of children are living in horrific conditions in the sewers and streets of these former communist countries. But now these children are being helped , through our Divine Mercy Foundation called H.U.D.T.

"Help Us Dry The Tears"

In the past few years, we have opened "House's of Divine Mercy" in many Eastern European countries.

We have spent over €200,000 on life saving operations on children, in the Marie Curie Children's Hospital in Bucharest.

We pay for accommodation, food, heating, and education for over 100 poverty stricken families in Romania.

We built an Educational Centre named after St. Faustina for children with long term illnesses in Bucharest.

We are building a church in Cupcini, Moldova which will be the first catholic church there since 1945.

We also have eight other mercy projects in hand, all under the patronage of St. Joseph.

Other Divine Mercy Publications

List of Bestsellers

Bkn19 - Mercy Sunday - The Gate to Heaven
Bk101 - Diary of St. Faustina
Bk103 - Handbook of Devotion to Divine Mercy
BK103- also available in Polish and Spanish
Bk104 - The Life of Saint Faustina
Bk107 - Guidelines for Divine Mercy Prayer Groups
Bk113 - She made an Ordinary Life Extraordinary
Bk115 - The Holy Cloak in Honour of St. Joseph
Bk117 - The Message of Merciful Love
Bk118 - The Everyday Miracles of Divine Mercy
Bk126 - The Colour Pieta
Bk127 - Pray the Rosary
Bk128 - Life Offering - Consecration to Mary
Bk129 - Rosa Mystica
Bk136 - Fatima Eucharistic Rosary
Bk147 - Holy Hour with the Merciful Jesus
Bk148 - Protect my Home and My Family
Bk150 - St. Brigid
Bk156 - Divine Mercy & Eucharistic Way of the Cross
Bk158 - The Eucharist - Church's Greatest Treasure
Bk183 - The Story of Saint Faustina
Bk184 - Medjugorje Messages 1981-2004
Bk189 - We Will Miss You - Tribute to John Paul II
Bk191 - Healing Prayers for the Sick
Bk200 - Angel on my Shoulder
Bk201 - Angel Prayers
Bk215 - Divine Mercy and the Real Presence
Bk216 - Mary, Lead Me, Guide Me
Bk217 - Sent Down from Heaven

Please Send for a Free Catalogue and Divine Mercy Newsletter
Divine Mercy Publications
Maryville, Skerries, Co. Dublin, Ireland
Tel: 00 353 1 8491458   Fax: 00 353 1 8492466
Email: info@divinemercy.org

John Morgans story is private revelation.
There being no conflict with the Church's teachings on faith or morals, we are free to believe or disbelieve these revelations.

Other Bestsellers

ANGEL ON MY SHOULDER VOLUME 1
(OVER 50,000 SOLD)

An old man's angel appears to him to help him save his soul

Bk 200 - Available from Divine Mercy Publications

After his evening meal John Morgan had a favourite spot in his garden, where he sat smoking his pipe and peacefully pondering life. At eighty-four years of age he had thought a lot about the meaning of life, of belief in God, and the existence of God.

Then one fateful evening he felt a presence, he turned to look and to his astonishment there was an angel standing at his shoulder.

After getting over the shock and he began conversation with the angel, the angel told him he was his guardian angel, and had come to answer the questions left unanswered in his life's search for belief in God.

ANGEL PRAYERS

This book brings together some powerful intercessions & protection prayers to our celestial friends.

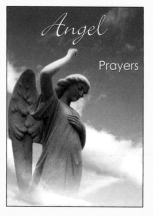

Bk 201 - Available from Divine Mercy Publications

They are there to fend off evil.
They are there to guide you.
They are there to keep you healthy.
They are there to make you wise.